STEPPING STONES:

A Guide to Knowing and Loving

Your Authentic Self

Ben Luskin, LPC, CPC

Cover Design and Interior Layout: Keli Keener

FROM THE AUTHOR

Welcome reader! I am filled with joy knowing that this book is in your hands. What you will find in the following pages is a collection of the many beliefs and mechanisms that helped me break free from the limitations of my perceived identity as "less than" and gain access to a life of abundance and purpose. Like my own ever-twisting journey through life, the book in front of you has evolved through many iterations on its way to its present form.

I created the blueprints for "Stepping Stones" on a snowy day in April, 2018. After hearing that my work was closed for the day, I sat down in my recliner, kicked out the footrest, and began retrieving and organizing the hodgepodge of recovery tools, techniques, and strategies that had been gestating in my mind for years. My process involved a synthesis of the aspects of humanity that I value most: personal integrity, honesty, and resilience; the themes of empowerment and ownership that had played such a vital role through my own recovery; and what I had learned about behavioral development through study and the myriad experiences from the varied roles I had filled in the social services field.

So you can probably imagine how many disconnected tidbits came flowing out of me that blustery day—suffice to say enough to create a 30+ lesson guide to recovery. Each time I moved to the next lesson, I somehow knew just what that subsequent step would entail. And then it was all over. My subconscious warehouse had been emptied. All the crowded shelves had been sorted through. As so often happens, the once-cluttered mess stored in my subconscious had become a somewhat less cluttered document stored on my computer.

It lay there for years, dormant, tucked away behind a file icon in the corner of my screen, until I dug it out from my database to use in the development of a support group for an alcohol use disorder platform. Though I had originally designed "Stepping Stones" specifically for brain injury recovery, I designed the curriculum to address an holistic understanding of self so it didn't take much to shift the content to a more general focus. I put in the legwork and was soon bringing "Stepping Stones" to life. What began as a generic weekly support group quickly grew into a thrice weekly dynamic gathering with its own culture and cast of characters. These meetings helped me understand better what worked and what didn't, and what made sense and what needed further clarification. It is now my great honor to share this work with you.

Sincerely,

Ben

Table of Contents

Introduction   7

Process Agreements   8

Personal Story   9

Awareness   13

Chapter 1   15

Mind-Body Connection   16

Self-Appreciation   18

Observation vs. Evaluation I   20

Observation vs. Evaluation II   21

Chapter 2   23

Spheres of Influence I   24

Spheres of Influence II   25

Behavior Mapping I   26

Behavior Mapping II   28

Chapter 3   31

Appreciate Past Self   32

Let Go of the Past   33

Accept New Self   34

Project 1: "I am..." poem   35

Discovery   37

Chapter 4   39

Visions of Success   40

Process vs. Outcome I   41

Process vs. Outcome II   42

Table of Contents

Chapter 5   43

The Way   44
Self-defeating Thoughts   45
Taking Risks   46

Chapter 6   47

Reinforcement   48
Relationships   50
Training Space   52

Project 2:   53
Draw "Self-In-Training"

Integration   55

Chapter 7   57

Time Continuum   58
Personal Values   60
Failure?   61

Chapter 8   63

Balance I   64
Balance II   65
Consistency   66
Renewed Personal Values   67

Chapter 9   69

Accountability   70
Worse Before Better   71
Supports   73

Project 3: Design   74
Integrated Lifestyle

You

Knows

You

Better

Than

Anyone

Else

Knows

You

Introduction

The group of you gathered here are about to embark on a difficult and tranformative journey together. While you arrive today as strangers, over the coming weeks you will be opening yourselves up and sharing your vulnerabilities with each other. You will also be discovering hidden strengths and opportunities that allow you to perform in ways that exceed your expectations. This process may lead to strong emotional connections as you begin to see each other as partners and teammates along your quest for personal greatness.

Note: The Stepping Stones curriculum can also be used individually.

Share 3 brief things about yourself that you believe accurately describe who you are.

Share what you hope to gain from the Stepping Stones curriculum.

Share any fears or anxieties you have regarding the work ahead.

Process Agreements

In order for us to make the most of our time together, we need to agree on what we expect from each other. But we can't hold fair expectations for others if we don't first clarify what we're asking them for. Consider what might make you feel safe and encouraged to challenge yourself in new ways, through the Stepping Stones curriculum, and in your daily life?

What do you need from others to feel safe and supported? How can you ask for that?

What can you do to show your support for others?

The Stepping Stones curriculum is comprised of 36 lessons divided into three phases: **Awareness**, **Discovery**, and **Integration**. Lessons are intended to be completed one at a time, allowing for material to be processed and absorbed. Each phase closes with a final project.

Limited space is provided below each question for you to take notes and write down short answers. Several additional pages are included in the back for overflow.

Many of the questions contain multiple prompts to stimulate thought and discussion. Please complete each question to your satisfaction. If no example is provided, answer the question according to how you understand it. There is no "right" way!

Personal Story

I'd like to begin our journey together by providing you with some self-disclosure. I am a severe traumatic brain injury (TBI) survivor who has faced a slew of challenges along my path of recovery. Though I may not have realized it at the time, my work in learning to overcome my challenges taught me so much of what I know about myself and the world today.

- When I was 12 years old, I sustained a severe traumatic brain injury when a semi-truck struck my family's minivan.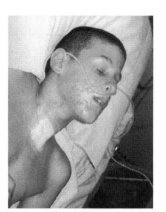
- I spent 6 weeks unconscious and 3 months in the hospital relearning how to walk, talk, and other basic skills.
- Throughout high school and college I struggled with self-acceptance, self-doubt, depression, anger, and more.
- My study of martial arts helped me recognize my self-worth, and showed me that I could learn new skills and overcome my perceived limitations through hard work, dedication, and repetition.
- I struggled with unemployment and the demands of being a new father.
- I developed an adaptive martial arts program called "Unleash the Beast: Primal Movement Workshop," based on 4 animal forms.
- I wrote my first book, <u>Beyond the Horizon: A Guide to Recovery from Brain Injury and Other Happenings</u>, presenting my ideas for empowerment-based recovery that would guide my future career development.
- As an advocate for empowerment in the field of mental health, I led workshops and presented at conferences around the country.
- I attained certification as a professional life coach and launched the first iteration of Launch Empowerment Mentoring oout of my garage.

- I joined the independent living (IL) movement and filled many roles over the years with a local center for IL, ranging from working in an acute psychiatric crisis ward to hosting a peer support club.
- I served on the Oregon State Independent Living Council (SILC) for 6 years, and was elected vice president for my last 3 years of service.
- I spent nearly a year fighting for my right to be an active father in my children's lives, during which I faced allegations of incompetence due to disability.
- Subsequently, I testified in front of congress in support of repealing legislation that included disability as grounds for termination of parental rights.
- I co-founded a local disability rights activist chapter.
- I served as quality-of-life consultant for a developmental disabilities provider agency and incorporated client empowerment into their program design.

continued

Personal Story

- I became licensed as a clinical mental health counselor in the state of Oregon.
- I built and ran a behavioral health program for the HIV+ population in Eastern Oregon.
- I was fired from my job as a behavioral health specialist for refusing to comply with a directive that contradicted my professional opinion of what would serve my client best.
- Within a month of being fired, I established a private clinical practice.
- I began leading several support groups on an online platform for alcohol use disorder (AUD).
- Most recently, I joined a medical response team providing mental health support to patrons at music festivals, joining my love for music and dancing with my passion for supporting others through their struggles.

By facing the challenges that have befallen me, I have learned to believe fiercely in myself and my potential. My practice of hard work, authenticity, and vulnerability has ensured that each step along my journey both strengthens my confidence in my intuition and helps me understand better how to share my personal gifts with the world. While I continue to struggle with self-doubt and feelings of inadequacy, I remain assured that my commitment to my personal values will lead me in the right direction.

When was a time you felt really good about your efforts? When did you feel like you showed up as the best version of yourself, aligned with your personal values and beliefs?

AWARENESS

An up-close look at where your behaviors come from

Chapter 1

Mind-Body Connection

Note: The following exercise may prove overwhelming and/or uncomfortable for certain individuals. If this is true for you, please make any accommodations you need to feel safe and secure.

At times, it can be difficult to slow down and focus on our needs and ways to fulfill them. When we are so consumed by the demands surrounding us, we can easily forget to take care of our own well-being. We may place ourselves as last priority. By raising our awareness of our physical body, we can better understand what we need to feel healthy and whole. We can begin to build a healthy, trusting, and safe relationship with ourselves, learning to listen and respond to our physical, mental, and emotional needs with compassion. A brief body scan or simply a period of silence and introspection can help us to redirect our thoughts from the outside world to our own needs. For this reason, I begin each Stepping Stones lesson with a full body scan and a few minutes of silence. You may choose to do the same. Below is a sample script:

I invite you to find a relaxed and seated position. Place your feet flat on the floor in front of you, about shoulder width apart. Scoot your butt back, straighten your back, pull your shoulders back slightly, and extend your neck. Most importantly, put intention into your posture. Hold your head straight and close your eyes or look downwards, whichever is more comfortable. Rest your hands comfortably in your lap. Breathe deeply, inhale and exhale. Take two deep breaths into each part of your body*, beginning with your head and moving down to your toes. Consider how each part of your body feels apart from the rest. What subtle sensations do you notice in each?

*head, face, neck, shoulders, upper arms, lower arms, hands and fingers, chest, stomach, waist, upper legs, lower legs, feet and toes, whole body

Now, breathe at your own pace and find your own rhythm. Maintain your awareness of your body and keep yourself grounded with your breath and your posture. Sit for five minutes, just noticing your thoughts and feelings floating by you, as if you are watching them through a window. Notice without judgement.

continued

The following exercise invites you to work with the physical sensations you noticed during the previous body scan and meditation. You may want to sit for an additional 3 minutes in silence to identify these sensations.

What did you notice in your body? Where did you feel it? How was the intensity? Did your sensations shift over time? Did they increase, decrease, or disappear?

Our bodies hold immeasurable wisdom and are sending us messages all the time. What messages do you think your sensations are telling you? How might these messages influence your future decisions?

Self-Appreciation

When we find ourselves dwelling on our struggles, we may quickly become fixated on our insecurities and lose touch with other parts of ourselves. During these times, it can be helpful to redirect our focus toward personal traits that we feel most proud of. In doing so, we can come to understand ourselves through a more inclusive and holistic scope, in which our vulnerabilities are framed within our strengths.

Yet, as we redirect our focus toward our personal strengths, it is just as important for us to honestly embrace our vulnerabilities. Both our strengths and vulnerabilities are integral pieces of the puzzle of self, without which the self is left fragmented and incomplete. This exercise asks you to take some time to appreciate yourself for exactly who you are. But first, let's look at an old Zen story that conveys this message well.

———————

The creatures of the forest were all gathered together one day, talking amongst themselves. Squirrel and Tiger were there, as were Spider and Butterfly. These creatures and many others were talking about their unique characteristics. Tiger was raving about how happy he was to be such a strong and fierce animal. Spider was telling the others how fortunate she felt to be such an artful weaver. Taking turns, one by one, each creature spoke about themselves. When it came to Butterfly's turn, she commented that she was so glad to have finally morphed from a caterpillar into a butterfly because she was sick of being stuck crawling around the dirt day after day. Upon hearing this, Worm interrupted and exclaimed "There is nothing wrong with crawling around the dirt day after day. I am a worm and that is all I will ever do. And that's OK because I love crawling around the dirt. I'm getting pretty good at it too!" Surprised by Worm's sudden enthusiasm, the other creatures thought for a moment and then nodded their heads in unison, signaling their agreement with Worm's point. Butterfly then commented, "yeah, when I was a young caterpillar I quite enjoyed crawling around the dirt. It wasn't until I started thinking about becoming a butterfly that I stopped enjoying the rush of feeling the cool earth across my body as I slithered around."

continued

Just like the worm in the story, we can accept and love ourselves for exactly who we are. Write down three reasons why you appreciate yourself in the space below. (If this is difficult for you, ask a friend for help.)

As you shift your focus to appreciating yourself, your autonomic nervous system responds by signaling safety and allowing your body to rest and heal. Take a few minutes now. Close your eyes, tune into your body, and think about the reasons why you appreciate yourself. What do you notice? What subtle sensations do you become aware of?

Observation vs. Evaluation I

The human mind is inclined to make quick assessments of the situations we find ourselves in. At one point in time, this ability was essential for survival. Contrary to our ancient ancestors, we now live in a time when our needs are often better met through careful consideration and planning. Shifting from the former to the latter involves slowing our minds down enough to distinguish what we sense (see, hear, touch, etc.) from the interpretations and judgments we attach to our sensations. In other words, we can learn to choose how we interpret the messages we hear from ourselves and others. We can learn to interact with the world proactively rather than reactively. We can learn to guide our behaviors with mindfulness rather than habit. The following exercise is adapted from Non-violent Communication (NVC).

Observations are factual: **neutral, clear, specific**, and **active...**

Ex. John arrived two hours after the meeting started.

Ex. Sarah told me that my joke hurt her feelings.

Evaluations are interpretive: **biased, vague, general**, and **passive...**

Ex. John is always late.

Ex. I'm a bad friend and I hurt people that are close to me.

Write down 3 observations of yourself:

_____

_____

Write down 3 evaluations you commonly make of yourself. For the purpose of this exercise, at least one should be a self-limiting evaluation.

_____

_____

Observation vs. Evaluation II Ch. 1:4

As you begin to distinguish observations from evaluations, you may find yourself dwelling in an unsettling space where meaning is fluid and ever-changing. As you consider that you are the one responsible for assigning meaning to your experiences in life, you may find yourself feeling overwhelmed and ill prepared. Remeber that with great responsibility comes great power. This in-between space where meaning is malleable can be a glorious land of opportunity.

———————•

Generally speaking, evaluations are observations conjoined with meaning. Consider one of your self-limiting evaluations from the previous lesson, or come up with a new one. Rephrase using this model: Observation + Meaning = Evaluation. What was the observation that led to the evaluation? What was the meaning you attached to the observation?

_____

_____

_____

_____

_____

Once you distinguish the observation from its attached meaning, you can replace that meaning with a new meaning—one that better matches your values and beliefs. Try for yourself. Take the meaning you identified above and replace it with a new one.

_____

_____

_____

AWARENESS

Chapter 2

Spheres of Influence I

We can better understand ourselves and our impact on the world around us by dividing our existence into 4 distinct spheres of relationship: relationship to community, relationship to family, relationship to self, and relationship to universe. In doing so, we can distinguish between traits that affect only one sphere, and larger patterns that overlap from one sphere to another. Even more, we can discover common theme(s) that show up in different spheres in our lives.

Similar themes may appear as strengths in one sphere and vulnerabilities in another. Through understanding the common source of these strengths and vulnerabilities, we can gain new appreciation for them. We can learn to incorporate them into our paths of recovery. Consider both your strengths and vulnerabilities within each of the spheres below. What comes easily, and where do you struggle in each sphere?

Relationship to Community

_____

_____

Relationship to Family

_____

_____

Relationship to Self

_____

_____

Relationship to Universe

_____

_____

As children, we hone our behaviors to meet the needs of our surrounding environment(s). Over time, these responses evolve into established behavior patterns that influence our construction of identity and our life direction. We tend to lean toward our strengths in meeting our needs, while avoiding our vulnerabilities whenever possible.

In simplified explanation, we build unique behavioral tendencies to accommodate three interrelated core needs: safety, connection, and self-worth—depending on numerous personal factors, each of us tends to favor one over the others. These behavioral tendencies figure prominently into our conscious as well as unconscious activity. In considering how your behavior has served your core needs in the past, you can better understand how your current actions, beliefs, and feelings relate to the satisfaction of these needs.

———•———

Looking through the behavioral traits you listed in the four spheres of influence in the previous exercise, can you identify any common themes between them? What core needs are these behaviors working to satisfy? What do you think is your predominant need?

_____

_____

Think of one or two pivotal experiences in your lifetime. How did these needs (and specifically your predominant need) show up? How did you satisfy them?

_____

_____

_____

_____

Behavior Mapping I

Our behaviors don't arise out of nowhere. Their roots can be found in our unconscious; in fact, some researchers place as much as 95% of the brain's activity in the unconscious! This means that the overwhelming majority of our decision-making process has been completed before we even become aware of the decision before us. The behavioral options available to us have already been sorted and picked through before they even arrive in our conscious mind. We are then left choosing between the few options our unconscious provides to us. And while we may not be able to select which behavioral options become available to us at any given time, we can learn to "stack the deck" so that the behavioral responses that agree with our intentions are on top, first to be drawn.

By breaking down how our behavior is transmitted from our unconscious to our conscious, we can gain insight into how our behaviors are satisfying—or not satisfying—our personal needs. We can understand better what is working well and what could use improvement. Ultimately, we can learn to smooth the transitions between each step in our process, allowing for our personal truth to guide every decision we make.

Intentions, Motivations, and Tendencies

Note: The terms "conscious", "subconscious," and "unconscious" are used within the context of the Stepping Stones curriculum and may or may not agree with other definitions assigned to the same terms.

Intentions — Our conscious intentions are the thoughts we understand in the here and now. They are specific and prompt us into action. For example, if I have the intention to eat, I will find some food.

Motivations — Our subconscious motivations connect our conscious intentions to our unconscious tendencies. They relate to the satisfaction of our personal needs. Referring to the example above, a motivation might be to eat so that I have energy to perform throughout the day.

Tendencies — Descending further, we find ourselves in the jungle of the unconscious. Here is where the roots of our behavioral patterns are found, derived from family and cultural influences as well as primal biological impulses. Our tendencies are the expression of our underlying beliefs about ourselves and the world around us. An example might be to associate fatigue with weakness.

continued

Behavior Mapping I

Intention

What are you telling yourself you want to do?

Ex. I want to exercise

Motivation

How are you fulfilling a personal core need?

Ex. Exercise satisfies my need to feel a sense of control over my life

Conscious
Intention

Subconscious
Motivation

Unconscious
Tendency

Tendency

What underlying belief(s) do you hold about this need?

Ex. I associate control with safety

Consider one or two of your everyday behaviors/activities. What are your intentions behind these behaviors? What motivations might lie behind these intentions?

Consider what tendencies might give rise to these motivations? Where else do you notice these tendencies in your life?

Behavior Mapping II

Sometimes our actions don't reflect our intentions. Sometimes we may even find ourselves behaving in contradictory ways. Referring to the previous model (Behavior Mapping I), the transmission from our subconscious motivations to our conscious intentions falls off track and is rerouted back to our unconscious tendencies, where mindfulness is absent. In these scenarios, our very understanding of right and wrong may be overshadowed by our ego's need for survival. In other words, our motivations can present in one of two ways: they can feed into our mindful intentions or they can collapse into our habitual tendencies. This juncture is represented by **Source**, **Surface**, and **Base** motivations.

Source, Surface, and Base Motivations

Source — This is where our motivations originate in response to a perceived personal need. The source has no expression of its own, but feeds into either surface or base.

    Ex. I need to feel a sense of belonging and connection.

Surface — Our surface motivations connect our subconscious with our conscious intentions. They are directed by mindfulness and reflect our chosen values and beliefs.

    Ex. I want to show my gratitude to my friend for their help through tough times.

Base — Our base motivations connect our subconscious with our unconscious tendencies. They are directed by habit and impulse and may disregard our chosen values and beliefs.

    Ex. I want my friend to like me more than their other friends.

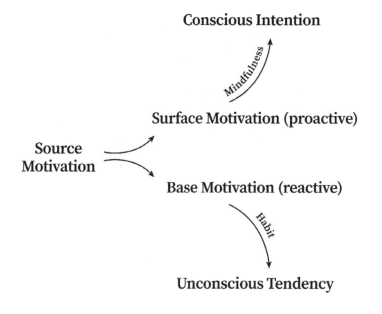

continued

Can you think of a time when your behavior did not reflect your intentions (e.g. self-sabotage)? What happened? What core need were you working to satisfy (source motivation)?

_____

_____

_____

_____

_____

What do you think was your base motivation driving this behavior? What might have been a better way to satisfy your core need? What is your surface motivation in this alternate scenario? (Remember that both your surface and base motivations stem from a common source motivation.)

_____

_____

_____

_____

_____

Chapter 3

Appreciate Past Self

Our previous accomplishments are not just a thing of the past. They can continue to bring joy and satisfaction into our lives indefinitely. Even if we feel like we have lost touch with the person we used to be, our past triumphs can remain as alive as ever through their influence on how we understand what we are capable of. In identifying common patterns among your past accomplishments, you can understand better how these patterns can continue to serve you.

If you're in a tough place right now, you may have come to the conclusion that you are no longer as capable as you once were. One of the greatest challenges along the path of recovery is letting go of your attachment to who you used to be, appreciating your past for what it was, and allowing yourself to move forward with grace into the future.

When were some moments that you felt accomplished in the past? What do they tell you about your strengths and vulnerabilities? How have they influenced your understanding of what you are capable of?

_____

_____

_____

Think about how your accomplishments have influenced your direction in life. What insights do you arrive at? What might this suggest about your future?

_____

_____

_____

Let Go of the Past

As difficult as it may be, releasing our attachment to the past can lighten our emotional load considerably. When we stop looking back at what happened and start looking forward to what could happen, we may feel a great sense of wonder and curiosity toward ourselves, our potential, and the world around us.

In the previous exercise, you considered where you find value in your past self. You took time to appreciate how certain qualities of that version of self have benefited you and how they continue to show up in your life today. Once you have honored this version of yourself as an integral part of who you are today, you can cease clutching to it as a thing of the past. By eliminating the duality between your past and present selves, you can release yourself from the confines (doubts, regrets, anger, etc.) of your past.

———————

Consider a challenge or ordeal that you have overcome in your life. What happened? What lessons or wisdom did you gain from that experience?

_____

_____

_____

How has this widom helped to bring you to where you are today? What has it helped you discover about yourself and the world? Where might this wisdom take you in the future?

_____

_____

_____

Accept New Self

Here is where you begin to build your new version of self. The previous lessons have given you some tools to assist you with such an immense project. In breaking down how and where your behaviors manifest, they have provided a map for you to understand how your core needs guide your direction through life.

As you leave your past behind and step into the future, you may find yourself unsure of who you are and what is important to you. You may find yourself questioning everything you thought you knew about yourself. In the midst of uncertainty, you can find comfort in your dedication to personal discovery and self-improvement.

•————————•

Consider why this work is so important to you? What do you value about yourself?

_____

_____

_____

What are you committing yourself to through the Stepping Stones process (routines, self-care, perspective shifts, relationships, etc.)?

_____

_____

_____

_____

Project 1

"I am..." Poem

In order to ground the discoveries you have made regarding yourself and your potential, the final project for phase one is to compose an "I am" poem. I encourage you to focus on how your understanding of yourself may have changed as a result of your work through phase one. A template is provided below. Have fun! Get creative and add an artistic touch if you feel so inclined.

Template:

I am _____

I come from _____

My life has taught me _____

I am most proud of myself for _____

I am capable of _____

_____

_____

_____

_____

_____

_____

DISCOVERY

An exploration of what a good life means to you

Chapter 4

Visions of Success

We learn from a young age to evaluate our behaviors according to standards defined by our families, cultures, and environments. As we grow older and develop our own unique sense of self, these standards become the framework for our understanding of self-worth and what it means to succeed. We celebrate when we meet or exceed these standards and lament when we fall short of them.

●————————————————————●

Who are some people in your life that you really look up to (e.g. family, political figures, social icons)? What qualities do you especially admire about them?

_____

_____

_____

_____

_____

Considering your response above, what does this suggest about your unique understanding of success? What kind of person do you aspire to become?

_____

_____

_____

_____

As we explore what success means to us, we can evaluate our efforts in relation to process or outcome. Whereas an outcome-based perspective holds a constant value, either positive or negative (or a mix of both), a process-based perspective is dynamic and forever evolving. So when we view our lives through the outcomes of our efforts, we are looking at endpoints; when we view our lives through process, we are looking at the journey from one point to another. Just as we can change our course if we see a traffic jam up ahead, we can make changes to our process if we don't like where it is leading us. No matter how difficult of a situation we find ourselves in, no matter how defeating the outcome of our decisions may seem during a moment, our process is what carries us forward and gives us opportunities to learn and grow.

Describe a time when you felt defeated by the outcome of a situation.

Thinking about the situation you described above, what needs were you trying to satisfy? How did you try to satisfy them? How do these needs show up in your life today, and what are you doing to satisfy them? How do your current efforts relate to your past efforts?

Process vs. Outcome II

All too often, we judge ourselves according to the outcome of our efforts and place little value in the efforts themselves. Even when we work hard at a task, we may feel disappointed when we don't achieve our desired results. Conversely, by evaluating ourselves according to what we put into our lives—rather than what we get out of it—we can experience a feeling of accomplishment moment by moment. We can gain a better understanding of our choices and what we can do to better our experience.

⎯⎯⎯⎯●⎯⎯⎯⎯

Consider an influential event in your life? What happened? How did it impact you?

How do you feel about your efforts during this event? Do you feel like you did everything you could to accomplish your desired results? What might you have done differently? What did you learn about yourself?

Chapter 5

The Way

When we direct our focus toward our process and away from outcome, we may discover that certain skills and strengths can be carried over from one activity to the next. Often, these personal traits are connected with our personal values. For example, one of my strengths is my ability to learn from my mistakes. I can bring this strength into any new activity I try. This strength is connected to my value of resilience. When we connect our process with our personal values, we can understand our every move in relation to how it promotes our personal values. We can feel more hopeful, motivated, and proud of who we are in each and every moment.

———•———

What is important to you about yourself and the way you show up in the world? What are three of your core values?

How do your values show up in your behaviors and life decisions? Try to think of one example for each value listed above.

What could you do to bring out your values even more?

As mentioned previously, one of our biggest obstacles to feeling good can be our own discomfort with feeling good. To avoid having to take responsibility for our decisions, we may unconsciously project our own self- defeating thoughts on to others. In other words, because a part of us feels inadequate, we may convince ourselves that others feel that way about us too. In other cases, we may direct our self-defeating thoughts toward ourselves, often as an expression of buried shame about who we are (or were). Through distinguishing our own thoughts about ourselves from what we think others think about us, we can gain insight into the source of our feelings of self-worth.

Describe yourself. What are your strengths, desires, and challenges?

Describe how you think your loved ones see you—your strengths, desires, and challenges.

How do the two descriptions compare? Where do you find similarities? Differences? What do your findings suggest about your feelings of self-worth?

Taking Risks

Thus far, we have explored shifting our understanding of our experience toward an effort-based, or process, perspective. Doing so allows us to understand even personally disappointing situations as successes. We can conclude that taking risks and placing ourselves in challenging situations can carry great potential for growth and development. As we learn to value our failures as well as our achievements, we can learn to see life as full of abundance and opportunity.

Risks come in many shapes and sizes. Some may seem so simple and mundane that you don't even recognize them for what they are. One of the most challenging risks of all is to be honest with yourself, to really listen to and do what you know is best for you. As difficult as it may seem to start down this path of honesty, the further you go, the easier it gets. Over time, you can learn to trust yourself and honor your intuition. In other words, taking the risk of being honest with yourself can help lead you to your authentic self.

Can you recall situations in your life where you took risks and learned valuable lessons? Think of one "success" and one "failure" that has influenced your personal development. What did you gain? What did you learn about yourself?

As you consider the risks you've taken throughout your life, do you notice a pattern? What does that pattern look like? Where can you find that pattern in your life today? How has it changed? How has it stayed the same?

Chapter 6

Reinforcement

We all learn from our experiences. Depending on how effective our behaviors are in fulfilling our needs, we learn to repeat, modify, or eliminate those behaviors. To encourage our learning process, we can implement positive and negative reinforcements. **Positive reinforcement** occurs when a stimulus is added in response to (or to encourage) a behavior. **Negative reinforcement** occurs when a stimulus is removed in response to (or to encourage) a behavior.

Reinforcements are tools you can use to support your growth. When you feel stuck or are struggling to make changes in your life, reinforcements can help you focus on taking small steps toward your goals. They can help you better connect your needs with corresponding behaviors.

———————

Consider situations in your life where you wish to change your behavior to better meet your needs. What are those needs? How are your current behaviors falling short?

_____

_____

_____

_____

_____

_____

_____

continued

Reinforcement

What alternate behaviors could you use to better satisfy the same needs? How could you use positive/negative reinforcement to encourage the new behaviors?

_____

_____

_____

_____

_____

How might your friends/family assist you with positive and negative reinforcement? How might you help them to help you?

_____

_____

_____

_____

_____

_____

Relationships

Our friends and family can offer us invaluable gifts along our road to recovery. By standing with us through our ups and downs, they can help us harness deep feelings of safety and love. The strength these feelings generate within us can help us (re)discover our love for and belief in ourselves. For those who have lost these relationships, even the memory of them can serve a similar purpose. Alternatively, relationships with animals and nature can offer similar benefits.

———•———

How have your friends and family supported you in your life? How have they influenced your understanding of yourself?

continued

Despite positive intentions, some of those closest to us may have a hard time adjusting to who we are becoming. In these scenarios, the responsibility lies with us to help them understand our transformation. With adequate time and effort, our loved ones may come to recognize our emerging potential.

There may also be individuals that for whatever reason are not able to accept us for who we are becoming. If this is the case, we can (at least temporarily) reduce or cease contact with them and move forward with grace, harboring no ill will. The common thread in each of these scenarios is that it is up to us to determine what is complementary to our growth and development.

———•———————•———

Can you think of a time when you advocated for your needs with another? How were you received? How has your life changed as a result?

Training Space

By establishing a designated training space, we can reinforce our wellbeing as a priority. This space can come to represent a safe space where the anxieties and doubts that show up in our everyday lives have no place. While in this space we may feel encouraged to identify with "best" versions of ourselves and we may discover that we can perform with greater skill than we previously thought possible. Ceremonies or symbols that represent personal strength can help to distinguish a training space from other spaces in our lives.

Training spaces can appear your life even if you don't recognize them. Their forms can vary from a physical location, a time during the day, a relationship, or an internal state or feeling. The critical element of any such space is the degree of intention that you put into it.

•————————•

How have you used training spaces in the past? How did they aid your growth and development?

Where and how might you establish a new training space in your life? How might you use How might it benefit you?

Project 2

You are now fully immersed in your process of transformation. Rather than considering who you are and what your life holds at present, you may at this stage feel more inclined to consider who you are becoming and what you want your life to look life in the future. So to finish off phase two, you will depict yourself in training.

Draw a picture, write a story, compose a song, or do anything else you can think of that depicts yourself in the process of training. Remember there is no right or wrong answer. Just let it flow!

INTEGRATION

A map for becoming the best version of yourself

Chapter 7

Time Continuum

Time is a constant in our lives; time always moves forward. Because of its consistency, viewing our lives through a context of time can help us to better understand how our behaviors today might impact our lives tomorrow, and how our behaviors yesterday have impacted our lives today. To aid in this task, I have broken time down into three dimensions.

Present — The present is our here and now, comprised of our sensory observations and perceptions of the world around us.

Imminent Future — This dimension holds the direct consequences of our behaviors.

Distant Future — Here is where the consequences from our imminent futures guide us into the next chapters of our lives.

———•———•———

When planning our path through life, it can be advantageous to consider both the direct consequences of our behaviors AND the long-term implications. By considering how our immediate decisions might influence our distant future, we can better understand how to guide our lives in desired directions. We can gather clues for how to create a chosen lifestyle and how to realize our best self.

To assist with this task, we can divide our aspirations into imminent goals and distant aims. Goals are typically easier to focus on than aims. They provide us with simple steps to take toward our aims. Set in the background and constantly shifting in relation to our personal growth, our aims can in turn help us to build on our accomplishments and establish continuity between our goals.

Goals — The challenges we set for ourselves in the imminent future. Goals are specific and can be measured. They follow the acronym SMART (Specific, Measurable, Achievable, Realistic, Timed). For example, a goal might be to run two miles two times in one week, or to spend five minutes sitting in silence before drinking coffee every morning for two weeks.

Aims — The dreams we hold for ourselves in the distant future. These often relate to the kind of person we wish to become. They can be abstract in design and are continually evolving. Referring to the examples above, related aims might be to complete a 15k race, or to learn to love oneself.

continued

What are one or more aims you hold for your distant future?

_____

_____

_____

_____

_____

What are some goals you can set for the imminent future that may lead you in the direction of the aim(s) you noted above?

_____

_____

_____

_____

_____

Personal Values

As you reemerge with your renewed sense of self and begin engaging with the world in new ways, you can look to your values for a sense of confidence and security. When you're not sure where to go or what to do next, your values can help to guide you toward what you "know" is best for you. Now that you have outlined some goals and aims to pursue, it is time to revisit your personal values, considering again what is important to you and what makes you feel the best about yourself. In the long run, alignment between your behaviors and values can assist you in accomplishing your goals, satisfying your needs, and achieving a strong sense of self fulfillment.

What are your personal values? List five:

How do your goals/aims reflect your values?

How might you modify your stated goals and aims to better reflect your values?

Try as we might, it is inevitable that we will struggle with and at times fail to accomplish the tasks we set for ourselves. Believe it or not, these failures can become some of the more valuable lessons in our lives. Not only do they offer us opportunities to learn from our mistakes, considering what worked and what did not work in previous attempts, but they can also teach us to forgive ourselves, pick up the pieces, and return with renewed strength and purpose. In other words, our failures can teach us invaluable lessons about ourselves and what we want out of life. They can help us to rearrange our priorities to reflect our personal greatness.

Can you think of a time when you learned valuable lessons from an experience of "failure?" What happened? What lessons did you learn?

_____

_____

_____

_____

What are some of your current struggles? How might you reframe these as opportunities for self-improvement?

_____

_____

_____

_____

Chapter 8

Balance I

As you begin to look holistically at your life and strive to build a self-fulfilling lifestyle, balance between your life activities can help you to feel stable and in control. To assist you in maintaining a healthy balance, you can divide your life into 4 (or more) categories: **Self-Improvement, Recreation, Responsibility to Others,** and **Rest/Self-Care**. While many activities may fall into multiple categories, distinguishing one category from another can help you to raise awareness of and focus on certain benefits of each. Sometimes a switch in perspective or a change in intention is all that it takes for a particular activity to fulfill different needs. For example, depending on the context, dancing (I love to dance!) can represent Self-Improvement, Recreation, or Self-Care.

⎯⎯⎯⎯⎯⎯⎯

Consider what self-improvement activities you currently practice that further your (1) physical, (2) mental, and (3) emotional learning? How do these serve you? What more could you add? Be specific.

_____

_____

_____

_____

Consider activities you do for recreation? How do these serve you? What more could you add?

_____

_____

_____

_____

In the last lesson, we looked at the categories of **Self-Improvement** and **Recreation**. The other two categories to consider are **Responsibility to Others** and **Rest/Self-Care**. Together, these four categories can help to ensure that your efforts in one area of your life do not leave you feeling exhausted and depleted, with little to give toward other opportunities that may arise. (You may find it helpful to revisit the introduction from the last lesson for a refresher.)

Consider what activities you currently practice in your life that involve responsibility to others. How do these serve you? What more could you do? Be specific.

Consider what activities in your life offer you opportunities for self-care. What activities do you practice to nurture yourself? What more could you do?

Consistency

Consistency, or following through with your intentions over time, is a critical factor in maintaining a balanced lifestyle. Like a muscle, consistency grows stronger through use. By selecting an activity—any activity—to commit to, you can hone your consistency. The nature of the activity you choose is insignificant compared to your level of follow through. Examples range from stretching each morning, to cleaning your room every Sunday, to returning phone calls from family/friends.

What does consistency mean to you in your life? How has it helped you?

_____

_____

_____

Where could you bring more consistency into your life? What might this look like?

_____

_____

_____

Describe an activity or behavior you can commit to following for 30 days.

_____

_____

At the risk of sounding like a broken record, I will say again that personal values can take a leading role in recovery. They can guide the direction of your life for years into the future. For the sake of this discussion, let us understand "values" as the parts of your life, which you consider the most meaningful. As you work to better yourself, you may notice your values shifting. For example, you might go from caring most about "not causing a scene" to "sticking up for what you believe in." So again, I invite you to take the time to consider how your values fit into the new identity and lifestyle you are creating. Perhaps with greater understanding and skill honed through the previous weeks, you will see new connections between your personal strengths, your lifestyle, and your underlying values.

————————

What was a significant experiences in your recent past that shifted the way you understand yourself and the world around you? How did this experience influence your understanding of your personal strengths and vulnerabilities?

How have your values shifted in response to your new understanding of self? What can you do to bring out these values even more in your life today, and in the future?

Chapter 9

Accountability

While it often gets lumped together with rules and order and thus gets a bad rap, **accountability** can be a great tool for helping you learn to respect and value yourself. It can help you stay in line with your values and on track with your intentions. Like consistency, accountability grows stronger with use. Throughout the Stepping Stones curriculum, you have been sharing with each other your personal thoughts and stories. In establishing a space that encourages honesty and vulnerability, you have perhaps unknowingly held each other accountable to do the same. In other words, the group has created an environment in which you all feel accountable to each other. Contrary to obedience, which is simply doing what you're told, accountability suggests a cooperative relationship between two or more individuals (or dimensions of self) in which expectations are established to guide performance.

———•———————•———

Where have you found accountability in your life? From yourself? From others? How has it served you?

_____

_____

_____

How might you use accountability to keep yourself aligned with your values, goals, and aims in the future? Be specific.

_____

_____

_____

Please understand that your life may get worse before it gets better. As you dedicate yourself to challenging your perceived limitations and accomplishing more than you previously thought possible, you will undoubtedly encounter resistance from yourself and/or others. Much of this resistance can be traced back to your ego. In other words, your ego will make excuses for itself to avoid having to face the hard truth of your situation: you are the only one that can truly make your life more fulfilling and enjoyable...and it takes hard work to get there!

We have already discussed the importance of including self-care in your life. Self-care includes all activities that help you feel better about yourself, including but not limited to physical exercise, eating healthy meals, and practicing self-forgiveness. At the root of these activities is belief in your own self-worth and your ability to improve your life.

In other words, we're talking about faith—faith in YOU!

Following is an apocraphyl interpretation of a story from the book of Exodus in the Old Testament. It illustrates just how crucial faith in yourself can be. Specifically, it shows how faith can provide the confidence and strength necessary to enter into unknown and frightening situations, and stay the course despite doubts and fears.

Note: The use of this story is parable and does not suggest any religious orientation.

The Israelites found themselves standing on the shores of the Red Sea, pursued by Pharaoh's army. They could not turn back, as they would certainly be slaughtered by the approaching soldiers, nor could they continue forward, as they would certainly drown in the waters of the Red Sea...or so they thought. Then one courageous individual stepped into the water and encouraged the others to follow. They kept walking forward, one foot after another, as the sea rose up around them. They kept walking forward, despite their fears, until at the very moment before the waters piled over them, the sea parted and cleared a safe path across to the other side.

continued

Worse Before Better

How do you identify with this story? What themes stick out for you? Can you think of a time in your past when your belief in yourself helped you get through a challenge?

_____

_____

_____

_____

_____

Where do you find faith or unwavering belief in your life today? How does it help you? What could you do to benefit even more from your faith?

_____

_____

_____

_____

_____

Supports

Even the strongest of us require assistance from others. As John Lennon and Paul McCartney so aptly wrote, "I get by with a little help from my friends." In working to build a new identity and follow your aims into the future, it can be helpful to consider the support you have in your life today. Supports come in many shapes and sizes. They may show up as friends and family, or as a passion for self-expression, or as deep devotion to an ideal. Ultimately, each of us can choose where we find our supports and how we use them. What we do with our supports determines how they can help us. You may be surprised to discover that your best supports come through giving, rather than receiving.

What does support look like in your life today?

What new supports would you like to add to your life? How might they help you achieve your goals?

How do you provide support for others? What more could you do?

Final Project

Congratulations!

You've worked through the entire Stepping Stones curriculum, answering questions and considering factors in your life that define who you know yourself to be. Now that you have a better understanding of and appreciation for yourself, you can create a lifestyle that reinforces your personal strengths and feeds your values. The final project asks you to create a framework for your balanced lifestyle, including activities that fit into the four categories we discussed—**self-improvement, responsibility to others, recreation, and self-care.** Be sure to also include means for **consistency** and **accountability.** Be specific.

For **Growth and Development,** I will include these activities in my daily/weekly schedule:

For **Responsibility to Others,** I will include these activities in my daily/weekly schedule:

For **Recreation,** I will include these activities in my daily/weekly schedule:

For **Self-Care,** I will include these activities in my daily/weekly schedule:

---

continued

Final Project

Means for **Consistency:**

_____
_____
_____
_____
_____

Means for **Accountability:**

_____
_____
_____
_____
_____

It's GO time!

There you have it, a rough outline for reclaiming control of your life. I have purposefully kept it brief and open for interpretation in order to leave ample room for you to customize your own path toward recovery. As long as you stay committed to your best interests, your process will ultimately yield rewards beyond what you can comprehend. (Remember what we have learned about understanding experience through personal reality and measuring success through effort.) At times those rewards may be difficult to recognize. They might look just like other disappointments in your life; yet given time to mature, they can sprout forth untold opportunities. Don't be fooled into thinking that any of this will come easily or that all your dark shadows and fears will suddenly evaporate once you begin your journey. Quite the contrary—your mind will likely become flooded with thoughts of "what if…" and "if only… ."

Each step forward may bring with it a new set of seemingly insurmountable challenges. During these times, which indeed will be many, you will be faced with having to make the hard decision to keep on going. You may find yourself reevaluating the meaning of your life and your existence. You may feel overcome with feelings of self-pity, asking repeatedly to no one in particular "why me?" If you feel discouraged by this grim picture, also know that your belief in yourself will grow every time you remind yourself, "yes, my life is worth fighting for!"

As your belief in yourself grows, so too will your ability to live in congruence with your personal values and aspirations. With this guide in hand, it is my hope that you will feel empowered to venture farther than you ever dared before. And sometimes that is enough. If each time you set out, you travel a little further; if each time you venture ouside, you stretch the boundaries of your comfort zone just a touch, over time your progress will become considerable. As my martial arts teacher Grandmaster Bong Pil Yang (n.d.) taught, water poured over a rock will splash off, but a steady drip will bore a hole through the same rock.

I have written this guide from the perspective of what has worked for me. Perhaps some of the tools shared will be of assistance to you and perhaps you will develop some of your own tools along the way. Regardless of the form of the tool, it is the person wielding it that determines the impact. That person is you. So no matter how difficult a situation you find yourself in, always remember that YOU are the authority of yourself. **No one knows better than you what is right for you.**

The first step is the most important. Once you begin, nothing and noone but yourself can stop you. So what are you waiting for?

Works Cited

Kaibara, Ekiken (1630-1714). Yojokun: Life Lessons from a Samurai, translated by William Scott Wilson. Tokyo: Kodansha International, 2008.

Lipton, B. H. (2016). The biology of belief: Unleashing the power of consciousness, matter, and miracles. 10th-anniversary edition. Carlsbad, California: Hay House, Inc.

Rosenberg, M. B. (2003). Nonviolent communication: A language of compassion. Encinitas, California: PuddleDancer Press.

Made in the USA
Middletown, DE
04 August 2024

58207819R00049